THE NEW NOVELLO BOOK *of*
SHORT & EASY ANTHEMS

For mixed-voice choirs

Selected and edited by David Hill

Novello

EXCLUSIVELY DISTRIBUTED BY

HAL•LEONARD®

Visit Hal Leonard Online at
www.halleonard.com

Contact us:
Hal Leonard
7777 West Bluemound Road
Milwaukee, WI 53213
Email: info@halleonard.com

In Europe, contact:
Hal Leonard Europe Limited
42 Wigmore Street
Marylebone, London, W1U 2RY
Email: info@halleonardeurope.com

In Australia, contact:
Hal Leonard Australia Pty. Ltd.
4 Lentara Court
Cheltenham, Victoria, 3192 Australia
Email: info@halleonard.com.au

THE NEW NOVELLO BOOK *of*

SHORT & EASY ANTHEMS

For mixed-voice choirs

Selected and edited by David Hill

NOVELLO

Published by
Novello Publishing Limited

Order No. NOV294393
ISBN 978-1-78305-415-2

This book © 2014 Novello & Company Limited.

Music processed by Paul Ewers Music Design.
Project Manager and Editor: Jonathan Wikeley.

Printed in the EU.

Introduction

Church and cathedral choirs have a deserved reputation for performing often-complex music to an extremely high standard, much of which they learn within an extremely limited rehearsal time. That said, there has always the need for short, simple anthems or pieces for reduced vocal forces – either for use as introits or communion motets, for smaller choirs, or on which choirs and directors can fall back in times of need. In many cases it can be all too easy to rely on a few stock pieces.

This book offers a new and generous selection of works for all occasions and times of year. While a few of the pieces may be well known, such as *View me, Lord*, by Richard Lloyd and Henry Ley's *A Prayer of King Henry VI*, there are many new works in this collection. All have been chosen with ease and speed of learning in mind. Some works such as Benjamin Britten's *Corpus Christi Carol* and Rupert Jeffcoat's ethereal *Weigh my heart* are for unison voices. Several, such as Alan Bullard's *Blest are the pure in heart*, call for reduced numbers of vocal parts, and many require only occasional simple four-part singing.

Several anthems provide interesting substitutes for other, more well-known works: choirs familiar with Anton Bruckner's *Locus iste* may wish to try his *In monte Oliveti*. Those looking for an alternative to Henry Walford Davies's *God be in my head* will find two contrasting versions here: by David Briggs and Herbert Howells. Peter Miller's beautiful miniatures *Lord, I am not worthy to receive you* and *Draw near with faith* can be used as an alternative to the Agnus Dei, or as effective communion anthems in their own right. *Heaven*, by Andrew Wells, with its optional solo quartet, offers an easy yet dramatic way to use the space of the church.

Some pieces provide useful anthems where there can appear to be a shortage of simpler works: James Davy's *And they shall beat their swords into ploughshares* is the perfect introit for Rogation Sunday, and Arthur Hutchings's infectiously boisterous *God is gone up* deserves to be better known as an Ascension Day anthem. Martin Baker's *Christus vincit* is a triumphant plainsong setting suitable for the feast of Christ the King.

This book hopes to convince that short and easy does not always mean mundane or over-familiar, and that many musical riches can be found in this necessary area of music to satisfy both choirs and congregations alike.

I am particularly grateful to my colleagues at Novello for their help, advice and expertise in creating this volume; in particular to Jonathan Wikeley for his editorial support, and to Sarah Lofthouse.

David Hill
Rutland, February 2014

Contents

Adam lay ibounden

Anon, c.1400
Sloan ms 2593

Andrew Cusworth (b. 1984)

took,___ As cler-kes find-en writ-ten in here book. *ah*___

Ne___ had the ap-ple tak-en been, the

ap - ple tak-en been, Ne had_ nev - er our la - dy a - been_ heav'-ne queen.___

Bless - ed be the time___ that ap - ple tak-en was! There - fore we moun sing - en:

Bless - ed be the time___ that ap - ple tak-en was! There - fore we moun sing - en:

Bless - ed be the time___ that_ ap-ple tak - en was! There - fore we moun

De-o gra - ci - as!___ De - o gra - ci - as!___

De-o gra - ci - as!___ De - o gra - ci - as!___

sing - en: De-o gra-ci - as! De - o gra - ci - as!___

Almighty God, which hast me brought

William Leighton (1565-1622)

Thomas Ford (*c.*1580-1648)

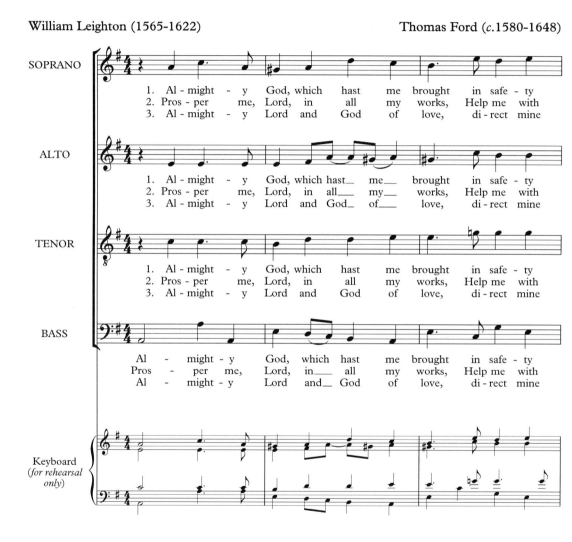

SOPRANO

1. Al - might - y God, which hast me brought in safe - ty
2. Pros - per me, Lord, in all my works, Help me with
3. Al - might - y Lord and God of love, di - rect mine

ALTO

1. Al - might - y God, which hast me brought in safe - ty
2. Pros - per me, Lord, in all my works, Help me with
3. Al - might - y Lord and God of love, di - rect mine

TENOR

1. Al - might - y God, which hast me brought in safe - ty
2. Pros - per me, Lord, in all my works, Help me with
3. Al - might - y Lord and God of love, di - rect mine

BASS

Al - might - y God, which hast me brought in safe - ty
Pros - per me, Lord, in all my works, Help me with
Al - might - y Lord and God of love, di - rect mine

Keyboard
(*for rehearsal only*)

Blessing

Lydia Smallwood

Ralph Allwood (b. 1950)

Blest are the pure in heart

John Keble (1792-1866)

Alan Bullard (b. 1947)

To Canon Chris Chivers

And they shall beat their swords into ploughshares

Isaiah 2: 4

James Davy (b. 1980)

Blackburn, 8 September 2006

Christus vincit

Worcester Antiphonal
12th century

arr. Martin Baker (b. 1967)

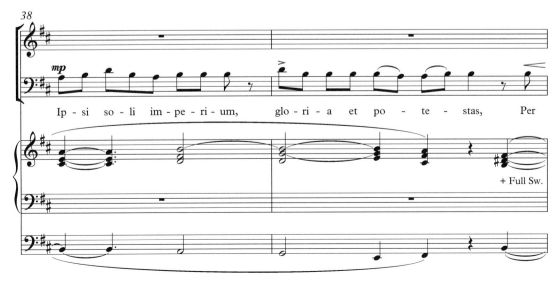

for John Hahessy

Corpus Christi Carol

from *A Boy was Born*

Words anon. (15th century)

Benjamin Britten (1913-76)

This carol has been arranged by the composer from his Choral Variations for mixed voices *A Boy was Born* (CH76549).
The words are from *Ancient English Christmas Carols* collected and arranged by Edith Rickert, and are reprinted by her
kind permission and that of the publishers, Messers. Chatto and Windus.

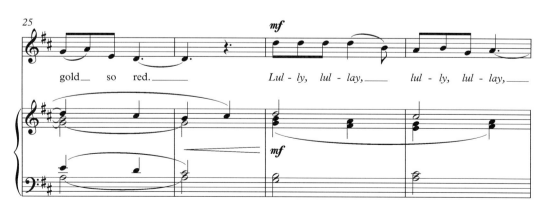

The fal-con hath borne__ my make*__ a-way. In that

or-chard there was__ an hall_____ That was hang-ëd with pur-ple and pall.__

And in that hall there was__ a bed,_____ It was hang-ëd with

gold__ so red._____ Lul-ly, lul-lay,___ lul-ly, lul-lay,___

* mate

rather f and animated

The fal-con hath borne_ my make_ a - way. In that bed there li -eth a knight,_ His wound - ës bleed-ing, day_ and night._ By that bed - side kneel-eth a may★,_ And she weep-eth both night_ and day._ Lul - ly, lul - lay,_ lul - ly, lul - lay,_

mf

Ped.

sim.

f broadly

f broadly and sustained

★ maid

The fal-con hath borne— my make— a - way.

And by that bed-side there stand-eth a stone,—

Man.

Cor - pus Chri - sti writ-ten there - on.—

ah— ah—

(without 4')

19 January 1961

Cradle Song

Isaac Watts
from *A Cradle Song*

Ashley Grote (b. 1982)

Gently rocking ♩ = 100

p 1. Hush! my dear, lie still and slum - ber, Ho - ly an - gels guard thy bed!
mf 2. How much bet - ter thou art at - tend - ed Than the Son of God could be,

Heavn' - ly bless - ings with - out num - ber Gent - ly fall - ing on thy head.
When from heav - en he de - scend - ed And be - came a child like thee!

pp 3. May'st thou live to know and fear him, Trust and love him all thy days; Then go

dwell for ev - er near him,

dwell for ev - er near him, See his face, and sing his praise!

dwell for ev - er near him,

Available separately from Encore Publications, Juglans House, Brenchley Road, Matfield, Kent, TN12 7DT, UK
www.encorepublications.com

Dedicated to Winston McAlister

Crux fidelis

Words attributed to
Venantius Fortunatus (c. 530–609)

Matthew Owens (b. 1971)

This piece may also be sung in unison by trebles/sopranos only.

Dul - ce li - gnum, dul - ces cla - vos,

RH: soft flutes 8'
LH: soft foundations 8'

pon - dus su - sti - net,

Dul - ce

su - sti - net.

(+ soft 32')

Edinburgh, 15 September 2003
revised, Wells, 22 January 2014

Draw near with faith

Invitation Prayer to Communion

Peter Miller (b.1946)

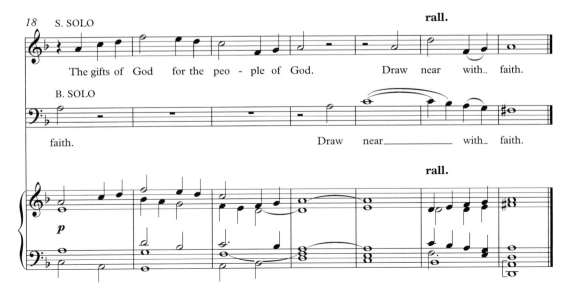

Es ist nun aus mit meinem Leben

Magnus Daniel Omeis (1646-1708) Johann Christoph Bach (1642-1703)

es ist nun aus, es ist___ voll- bracht,
Nun ist es aus, es ist___ voll- bracht,
Mein Leid ist aus, es ist___ voll- bracht,
Was Je - sus macht, is wohl - ge - macht!

Welt, gu - te Nacht!

Welt, gu - te Nacht! Welt, gu - te Nacht!___ Welt, gu - te Nacht!

1. Now my life is ended,
God who gave it, takes it to him.
Not the smallest drop remains in the vessel,
no faint spark will now avail it, life's light
is extinguished. Not the least grain of sand
still runs through the glass,
it is now ended, it is accomplished,
world, good night!

2. Come, day of death, o sun of life,
you bring me more joy and bliss
than the day of my birth can bring,
you put an end to my suffering,
which before the joys of christening
was already begun.
Now it is ended, it is accomplished,
world, good night!

3. World, good night! Keep what is yours,
and leave Jesus as mine own,
for I will not leave my Jesus!
May God protect you, my dear ones,
let my death not grieve you,
since it has brought me such happiness;
my suffering is ended, it is accomplished,
world, good night!

4. Why would you grieve for me?
Ah, ease your tears,
for mine are eased already;
Jesus wipes them from my eyes;
what use then should yours be,
laugh with me like a child.
That which Jesus does is well done!
World, good night!

for the Choir of Packwood Parish Church, Warwickshire

God be in my head

Richard Pynson
Horae BVM, 1514

David Briggs (b. 1962)

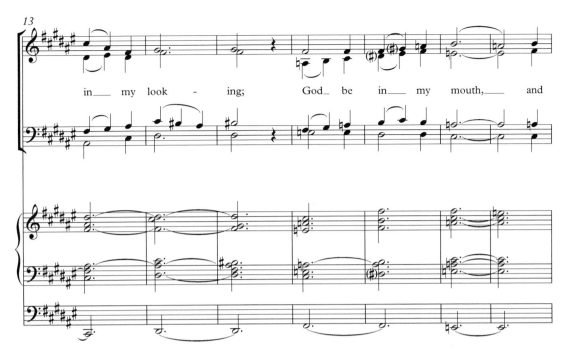

in___ my look - ing; God_ be in___ my mouth,___ and

in___ my speak - ing; God_ be in___ my heart,___ and

in___ my think - ing; God be at___ mine end,___

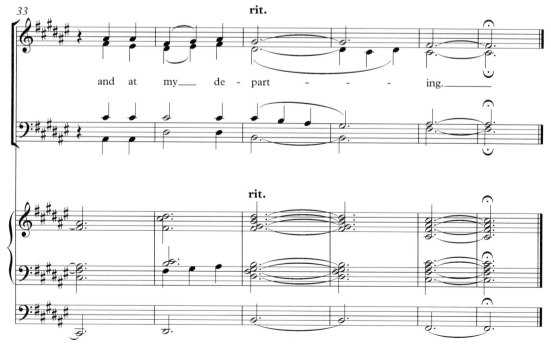

and at my___ de - part - - - ing.___

New York, February 2005

For the Fallen

Laurence Binyon (1869-1943)

David Terry (b. 1975)

5 November 2013

God is gone up

Psalm 47: 5 & 6
Psalm 68: 18

Arthur Hutchings (1906-1989)

Brisk and vigorous ♩ = 112

This piece may be sung up a tone.

Hear my voice, O Lord

Psalm 27: 9, 11, 12 & 17

Rupert Jeffcoat (b. 1970)

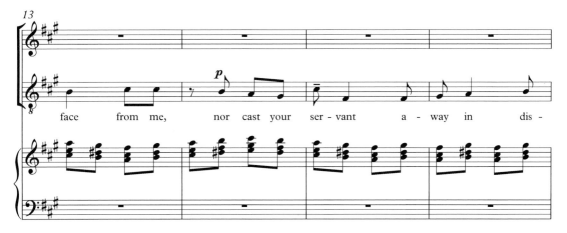

face from me, nor cast your ser - vant a - way in dis -

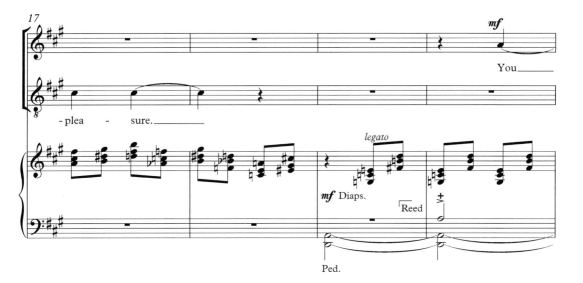

- plea - sure. You

legato

mf Diaps.

Reed

Ped.

have been my help - er; leave me not, nei - ther for -

leave me not, nei - ther for -

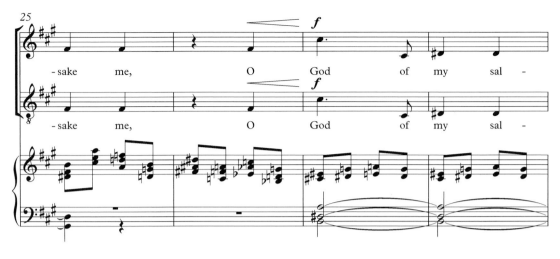

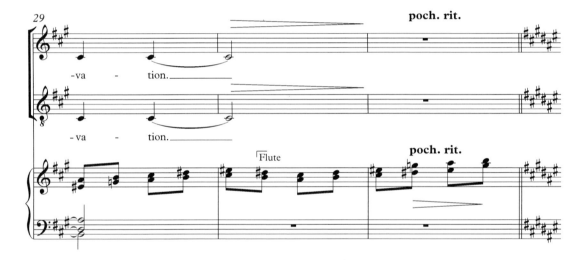

for Celia Harper and Chiswick Baroque

Heaven

George Herbert (1593-1633)

Andrew Wells (b. 1962)

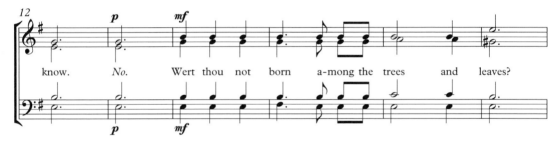

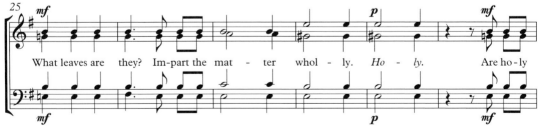

* Echoes can be sung full or by a solo quartet in a separate part of the church.

leaves the e – cho then of bliss? *Yes.* Then tell me,

what is that su - preme de – light? *Light.* Light of the mind: what shall the

will en - joy? *Joy.* But are there cares and bus – 'ness with the

plea – sure? *Lei – sure.* Light, joy, and lei – sure;

meno mosso

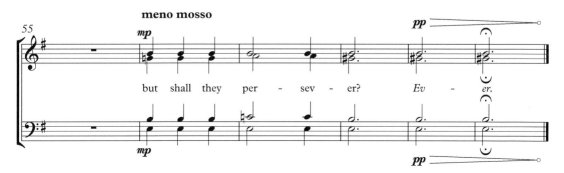

but shall they per – sev – er? *Ev – er.*

God be in my head

Richard Pynson
Horae BVM, 1514

Herbert Howells (1892-1983)
ed. Patrick Russill

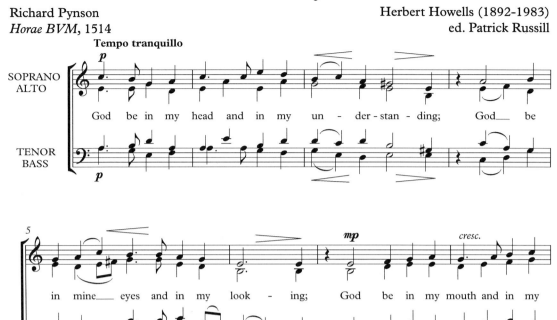

God be in my head and in my un-der-stan-ding; God be
in mine eyes and in my look-ing; God be in my mouth and in my

speak-ing; God be in my heart and in my think-ing;

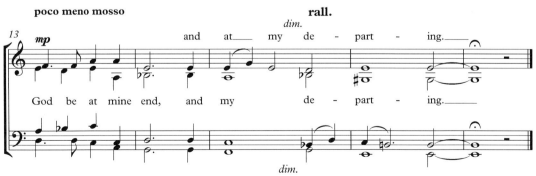

and at my de-part-ing.
God be at mine end, and my de-part-ing.

I sing of a maiden

15th-century English carol

Lennox Berkeley (1903–1989)

$_1$ *makeless* = matchless
$_2$ *ches* = chose

In the departure of the Lord

William Leighton (1565-1622)

John Bull (1562-1628)

Transposed up a tone.

In monte Oliveti

Matthew 26: 39

Anton Bruckner (1824-1896)

In mon-te O-li-ve-ti o-

-ra-vit ad Pa- trem: Pa-ter, si fi-e-ri

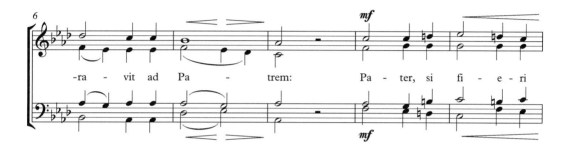

po- test, tran-se-at a me ca-lix i- ste:

Fi-at vo-lun-tas___ tu-a, vo-lun-tas tu- a.

To Julia and Jack Mitchener from The Adult Choir, St. Paul's Episcopal Church, Winston-Salem, NC
8 June 2008
In celebration of their ministries at St. Paul's as they prepare to move to Ohio

The Lord bless you and keep you

Numbers 6: 24-26

Dan Locklair (b. 1949)

24 May 2008
Winston-Salem, NC

Lord, I am not worthy

Invitation Prayer to Communion

Peter Miller (b. 1946)

Lord, I am not wor-thy to re-ceive you but on-ly say the
God, who takes a - way the sins of the world.

word and I shall be healed. Lord, I am not
Hap - py are those who are called to his sup-per.
Hap - py

The organ may join in at this point.

(rich and warm)

Ped. 16'

wor-thy to re-ceive you, but on-ly say the word and I shall be healed.

The Lord's Prayer

from the *Liturgy of St. John Chrysostom*, Op.41

tr. Alexander Milner

Pyotr Ilyich Tchaikovsky (1840-1893)

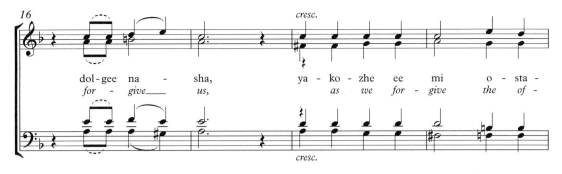

dol - gee na - sha, ya - ko - zhe ee mi o - sta -
for - give___ us, as we for - give the of -

- vlya - yem dolzh-nee-kom na - shim. Ee nye vye-dee nas vo ees-koo -
- fenc - es of our e - ne - mies. And do not lead us in - to temp -

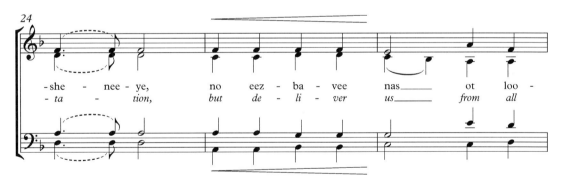

- she - nee - ye, no eez-ba-vee nas___ ot loo -
- ta - tion, but de - li - ver us___ from all

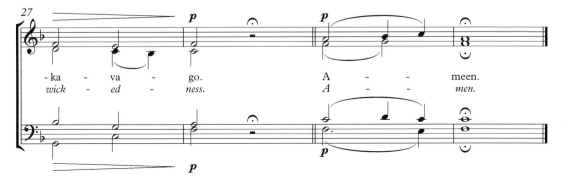

- ka - va - go. A - - meen.
wick - ed - ness. A - - men.

Miserere mei

from Psalm 51

Henry Purcell (1659-95)
ed. Anthony Lewis and Nigel Fortune

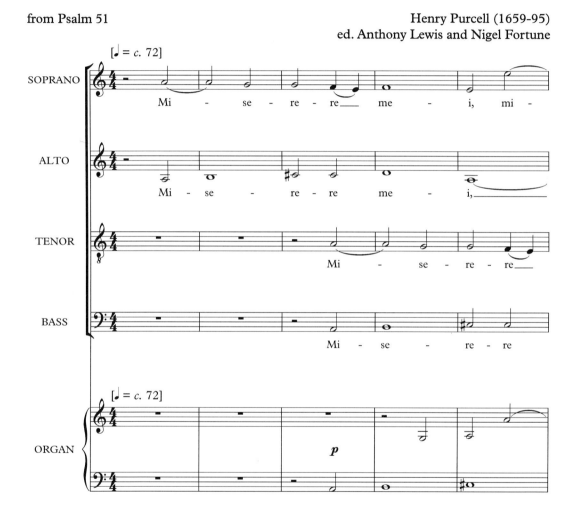

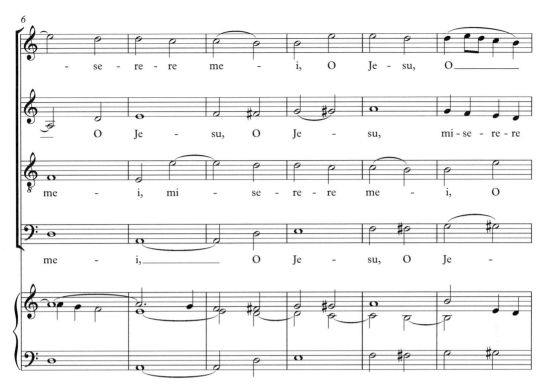

Mother of God, here I stand

Mikhael Lermontov (1814-1841)   John Tavener (1944-2013)

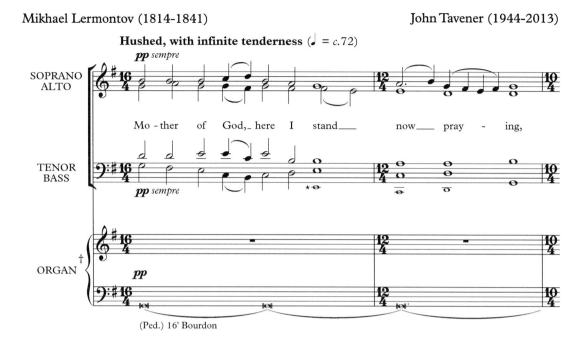

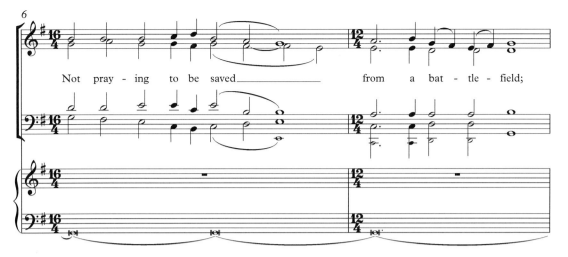

Not pray - ing to be saved_____ from a bat - tle - field;

Not giv - ing__ thanks, nor seek - ing for - give - - - ness

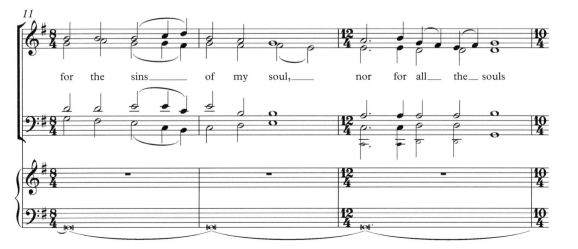

for the sins____ of my soul,___ nor for all__ the__ souls

Numb, joy - less and de - so - late on earth;

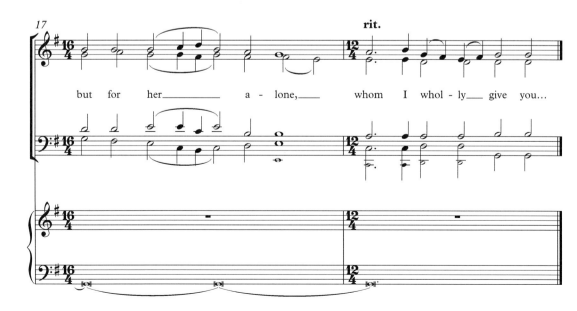

rit.

but for her_____ a - lone,_____ whom I whol - ly___ give you...

My Jesu, sleep

Rev. H. R. Bramley (1833-1917)

Adam Harvey (b. 1964)

Tenor solo / choir hum

'O lamb, my love inviting,
O star, my soul delighting,
O flower of mine own bearing,
O jewèl past comparing!
My darling, do not weep, my Jesu, sleep!'

Soprano solo / choir hum

'My child, of might indwelling,
My sweet, all sweets excelling,
Of bliss the fountain flowing,
The dayspring ever glowing!
My darling, do not weep, my Jesu, sleep!'

Full

'My joy, my exultation,
My spirit's consolation;
My son, my spouse, my brother,
O listen to thy mother!
My darling, do not weep, my Jesu, sleep!'

For David Scott-Thomas and the gentlemen of Blackburn Cathedral Young People's Choir
To my mother on her ordination, September 24th, 2006

O salutaris Hostia

Thomas Aquinas (1225-1274)

James Davy (b. 1980)

R. *Flûte, Gambe, Voix Celeste,*
(et Bourdon, Voix Humaine et
Tremolo où praticable)

P. *16' Bourdon,*
R/Ped.

O for a lay!

George Ratcliffe Woodward (1848-1934)

Melody: Bohemian Brethren, 1566
harm. Charles Wood (1866-1926)

1. O for a lay! For on this day, This day, the first of the se - ven,
2. Fair was the morn when Christ was born, But fair-er yet is the mor - row,
3. So, man, re-joice, up-lift thy voice, Al - le, al-le, al-le-lu - ia.

Christ is re-stored to life, the Lord, Mo - narch of earth and of hea - ven.
When from the dead up - rose our Head, End - ing our night-time of sor - row.
Sooth - ly 'tis time to clang the chime, Al - le, al-le, al-le-lu - ia.

De - feat-ed hell, and death as well, On Ea-ster E'en our God is seen
And from the light of Eas - ter bright We, ash and dust, sure hope and trust
Sirs, pray you sing to Christ our King, Who, late - ly slain, is ris'n a - gain;

Stand - ing a - mid the E - le - ven.
Of our a - gen - ris - ing bor - row.
Al - le, al-le, al - le - lu - ia.

A Prayer of King Henry VI

King Henry VI (1422-71)

Henry G. Ley (1887-1962)

Composed for the Royal Foundations of King Henry VI at Eton College and King's College, Cambridge (1928)

*The printed accents denote a word stress
**If desired this introit may be sung in the plural

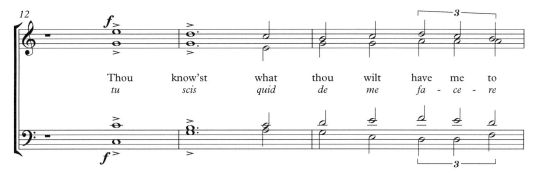

Thou know'st what thou wilt have me to
tu scis what quid de me fa - ce - re

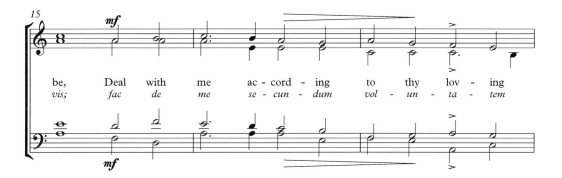

be, Deal with me ac - cord - ing to thy lov - ing
vis; fac de me se - cun - dum vol - un - ta - tem

Very slowly

kind - - ness, And show me thy
tu - - am cum mi - se - ri -

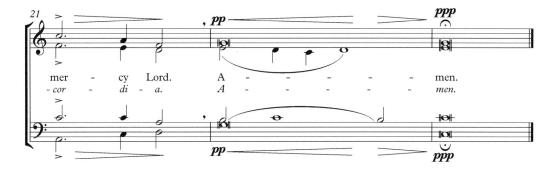

mer - cy Lord. A - - - - - men.
-cor - di - a. A - - - - men.

O salutaris Hostia

Thomas Aquinas (1227-1274)

David Terry (b. 1975)

for Benjamin Nicholas and the choir of the Abbey School, Tewkesbury

The Two Adams

John Donne (1572-1631)

from *Hymn to God, my God, in my Sickness*

Christopher Borrett (b.1985)

In loving memory of James Edward Colling Allen

A Thin Place

Words and music:
Jonathan Wikeley (b. 1979)

This piece may also be sung at Christmas, substituting the words 'Where Jesus Christ is born' in bars 32-34.

place:_____ Where God stretch-es out his hand, And we___ but

thin place, this is a thin place, this is a thin place,

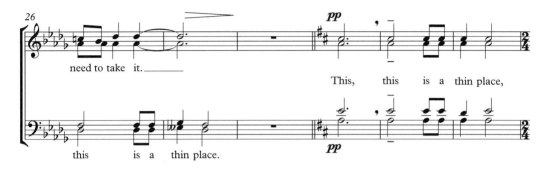

need to take it._____

This, this is a thin place,

this is a thin place.

Where Christ our Lord is ris'n, And ev' - ry-thing, ev' - ry-thing,

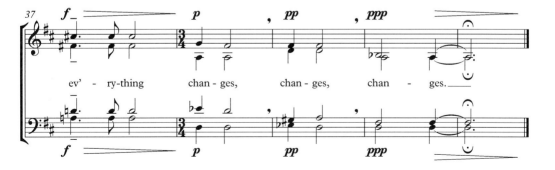

ev' - ry-thing chan - ges, chan - ges, chan - ges._____

For the Church of St Peter's, Hammersmith

Tu es Petrus

Matthew 16: 18

Andrew Wells (b.1962)

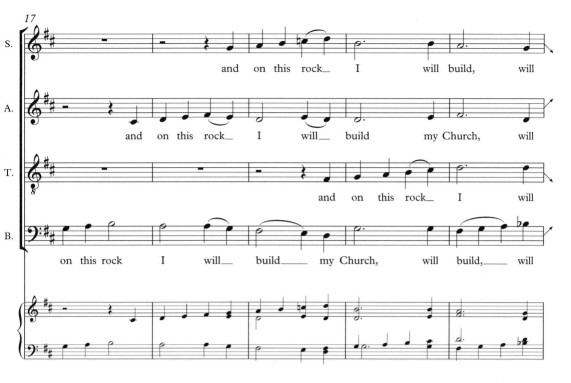

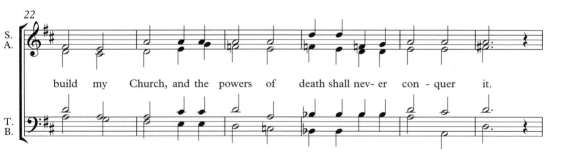

For M. M.

View me, Lord

Thomas Campion (1567–1620)

Richard Lloyd (b. 1933)

1. View me, Lord, a work of thine: Shall I then lie drown'd in night? Might thy grace in me but shine, I should seem made all of light.

2. Cleanse me, Lord, that I may kneel At thine al - tar, pure and white; They that once thy mer - cies feel, Gaze no more on earth's de - light.

3. World - ly joys, like sha - dows, fade___ When the heav'n - ly light ap - pears;

But the cov-'nants thou hast made,___ End - less,___ know nor days, nor years.

4. In thy word, Lord, is my trust,___ To thy mer-cies fast I fly; Though I

am but clay and dust,___ Yet___ thy___ grace can lift me high.

Weigh my heart

Psalm 17: 3, 6 & 8

Rupert Jeffcoat (b. 1970)

Why fum'th in fight

No. 3 from *Nine Tunes for Archbishop Parker's Psalter*

Matthew Parker (1504-1575)

Thomas Tallis (1505-1585)
Ed. David Skinner

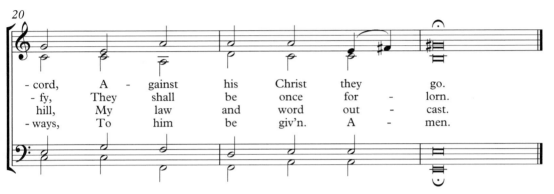

DEC. 7. God's words decreed, I, Christ, will spread
For God thus said to me:
My Son I say, thou art this day,
I have begotten thee.

CAN. 8. Ask thou of me, I will give thee,
To rule all Gentiles' lands:
Thou shalt possess, in sureness
The world how wide it stands.

DEC. 9. With iron rod, as mighty God,
All rebels shalt thou bruise:
And break them all, in pieces small,
As shards the potters use.

CAN. 10. Be wise therefore, ye kings the more,
Receive ye wisdom's lore:
The judges strong, of right and wrong,
Advise you now before.

DEC. 11. The Lord in fear, your service bear,
With dread to him rejoice:
Let rages be, resist not ye,
Him serve with joyful voice.

CAN. 12. The Son kiss ye, lest wroth he be,
Lose not the way of rest:
For when his ire is set on fire,
Who trust in him be blest.

Doxology. (FULL)

Veni creator

Song 44

George Wither (1588-1667)

Orlando Gibbons (1583-1625)
Ed. David Skinner

9
from, Oh, fill them with thy heav - 'nly grace. Thou
old; Our tongues en - rich - ing by the Word. Oh!
so We ev - 'ry dan - ger may es - chew. Let
To
from, Oh, fill them with thy heav - 'nly grace. Thou
old; Our tongues en - rich - ing by the Word. Oh!
so We ev - 'ry dan - ger may es - chew. Let
To
from, Oh, fill them with thy heav - 'nly grace. Thou
old; Our tongues en - rich - ing by the Word. Oh!
so We ev - 'ry dan - ger may es - chew. Let
To
from, Oh, fill them with thy heav - 'nly grace. Thou
old; Our tongues en - rich - ing by the Word. Oh!
so We ev - 'ry dan - ger may es - chew. Let
To
13
art that com - fort from a - bove, The high - est doth
give our blind - ed sen - ses light; Shed love un - to
us be taught the bless - ed Creed Of Fa - ther, and
thee, the Fa - ther, and the Son: (Whom past and pre -
art that com - fort from a - bove, The high - est doth by
give our blind - ed sen - ses light; Shed love un - to each
us be taught the bless - ed Creed Of Fa - ther, and of
thee, the Fa - ther, and the Son: (Whom past and pre - sent
art that com - fort from a - bove, The high - est doth by
give our blind - ed sen - ses light; Shed love un - to each
us be taught the bless - ed Creed Of Fa - ther, and of
thee, the Fa - ther, and the Son: (Whom past and pre - sent
art that com - fort from a - bove, The high - est doth
give our blind - ed sen - ses light; Shed love un - to
us be taught the bless - ed Creed Of Fa - ther, and
thee, the Fa - ther, and the Son: (Whom past and pre -

17

by gift im - part; Thou spring of life, a fire of
each heart of our, And grant the bod - ies fee - ble
of Son, by three And how from both thou dost pro -
- sent times a - dore) The one in three, and three in

___ gift im - part; Thou spring of life,___ a fire of
___ heart of our, And grant the bod - ies fee - ble
___ Son, by three And how from both___ thou dost pro -
___ times a - dore) The one in three,___ and three in

_____ gift im - part; Thou spring of___ life,_____ a fire of
_____ heart of our, And grant the___ bod - - ies fee - ble
_____ Son, by three And how from___ both_____ thou dost pro -
_____ times a - dore) The one in___ three,_____ and three in

by gift im - part; Thou spring of life, a fire of
each heart of our, And grant the bod - ies fee - ble
of Son, by three And how from both thou dost pro -
- sent times a - dore) The one in three, and three in

21

love, And the an - oint - ing spi - rit art:
plight, May be en - a - bled, by thy pow'r.
- ceed, That our be - lief it still may be.
one, All glo - ry be for ev - er - more.

love, And the an - oint - ing ____ spi - rit art:
plight, May be en - a - bled, ____ by thy pow'r.
- ceed, That our be - lief it ____ still may be.
one, All glo - ry be for ____ ev - er - more.

love, And the an-oint - ing____ spi - rit art:
plight, May be en - a - bled,____ by thy pow'r.
- ceed, That our be - lief it____ still may be.
one, All glo - ry be for____ ev - er - more.

love, And the an - oint - ing spi - rit art:
plight, May be en - a - bled, by thy pow'r.
- ceed, That our be - lief it still may be.
one, All glo - ry be for ev - er - more.